**图书在版编目（ＣＩＰ）数据**

圣迹之图/山东省曲阜市文物管理委员会供稿．-济南：
山东友谊出版社，1999.9重印
ISBN 7-80551-114-4

Ⅰ．圣…　Ⅱ．山…　Ⅲ．连环画-中国-现代　Ⅳ．J228.4

中国版本图书馆CIP数据核字（1999）第41373号

# 聖蹟之圖

山東省曲阜市文物管理委員會供稿

山東友誼出版社

# The Pictures about Confucius Life

by Qufu Administrative
Commission of the Culture Relics of Shandong

Shandong Friendship Press

# 前　言

《聖蹟之圖》是一部反映孔子生平事跡的連環圖畫。

孔子，名丘，字仲尼，春秋時期魯國陬邑昌平鄉（今山東省曲阜市東南尼山附近）人，是我國歷史上偉大的思想家、政治家、教育家。

孔子的先世本爲宋國公族，曾祖防叔爲躲避華督之亂遷到魯國，父親叔梁紇爲魯國陬邑大夫。孔子生於周靈王二十一年（魯襄公二十二年，公元前五五一年）十月庚子（今農歷八月二十七日）三歲時父親去世，家道中落，隨母親顏徵在遷居魯國都城內。在家庭及社會環境的熏陶下，孔子自幼年即虛心向學，他「俎豆禮容」，「十有五而志於學」，「學而不厭」「敬而好學，不恥下問」。少時貧寒，曾擔任過委吏（管倉庫）、乘田（管畜牧）等小官吏。中年開始聚徒講學，從事教育活動。他主張有教無類，首開私人講學之風，改變了學在官府的局面，打破了貴族對教育的壟斷，把文化教育推行到民間。五十歲前後從政，先後擔任過魯國的中都宰、司空（主管國家建設）、司寇（主管國家刑罰），幾年後辭職周遊列國，宣傳自己的政治主張，尋求實現自己理想的機會。他棲棲遑遑，席不暇暖，到處奔波，奔走於衛、曹、宋、陳、蔡、楚等國。但是，他的主張並沒有被各國執政者所採納「削跡於衛，伐樹於宋，窮於商周，厄於陳蔡」到處碰壁。晚年返歸魯國，潛心整理古代文化典籍，刪詩書，定禮樂，修春秋，贊周易。周敬王四十一年（魯哀公十六年，公元前四七九年）四月乙丑（今農歷二月十八日）賫志以歿，死後葬於「魯城北泗上」。

孔子一生對人類做出了重大貢獻，爲後人提供了一份珍貴的文化遺產。他整理古代文化典籍，獻身教育事業。一生如饑似渴地追求知識，學思結合，治學嚴謹，是後人學習的榜樣。他的貢獻還在於創立了儒家學派。他主張仁者愛人，提倡忠恕之道，主

張德治教化，反對苛政和任意刑殺。孔子生前沒有被統治者所看重，他創立的儒家學說也未受到重視，漢代「罷黜百家，獨尊儒術」以後，統治階級對孔子思想不斷改造，使孔孟之道成爲中國封建社會的正統思想，孔子也被推崇爲「大成至聖先師」，奉爲「萬世師表」。

爲表達對孔子的崇敬、懷念，從漢代起，人們就開始塑造能夠訴諸於視覺的孔子形象。東漢光和元年（一七八年）京城「置鴻都門學，畫孔子及七十二弟子像」，山東嘉祥武梁祠也有了反映孔子覺老子的畫像石刻。曲阜孔廟在北朝時就「有夫子像，列二弟子執卷立侍」，東魏興和元年（五三九年）又塑孔子像，列十弟子從侍。北宋時，孔廟又增加了臨摹的相傳晉代顧愷之繪隨行像，唐吳道子繪小影以及行教像、司寇像石刻，爲反映孔子行踪的《聖蹟之圖》的出現開了先聲。

《聖蹟之圖》約出現於明代，有彩繪本、木刻本、石刻本。

本冊《聖蹟之圖》是彩繪絹本，共三十六幅，紙裱成册。每頁闊六十六點二厘米，高四十一點四厘米，畫心闊五十七至六十二厘米不等，高近三十三厘米，無款，作者不詳，繪制年代也不詳。圖前有二跋，清世宗雍正七年（一七二九年）跋認爲出自明代成化弘治（一四六五年—一五〇五年）年間，此說是比較可信的。

《聖蹟之圖》有確切年代的是石刻，明萬歷二十年刊。据《聖圖殿記》說，「闕裏故有聖蹟圖若干幅，在棗梨，……散在各廡」。萬歷十九年山東巡按御史何出光倡議將木刻改爲石刻，並於孔廟寢殿後創蓋聖圖殿加以保存。翌年，山東按察副使張應登按部到曲阜，建議增加「克復傳顏」、「孝經傳曾」、「合葬於防」、「過庭詩禮」、「望吳門馬」、「杏壇植檜」、「三壟植楷」等，將圖增至一百一十二幅。彩繪《聖蹟之圖》與石刻相對照，僅「在齊聞韶」一幅爲石刻所無；「因膰去魯」、「丑次同車」各爲二幅畫面，但文字只在一幅上。三十六幅畫面絕大部分相同或基本相同，如「漢高祀魯」一幅，石刻只比彩繪減少了高祖背後的武士二人，文字

減去了贊語，添加了題目：「治任別歸」，僅刪去了左上角樹木及

文字贊語：「歸田謝過」雖略有差異，但畫面僅刪去左下角小橋

等景物。這說明彩繪《聖蹟之圖》與石刻《聖蹟之圖》有一定的

淵源關係，或者二者都以孔廟舊存木刻為底本，或者彩繪本就是石

刻的底本，但是石刻斷不能是彩繪的底本。這是因為：一，石刻

比彩繪構圖更為集中，如前舉「丑次同車」，彩繪作二幅，石刻合

為一幅，畫面選擇靈公夫婦同乘、孔子慚而欲去的瞬間；二，石

刻每幅均有四字題目，較彩繪醒目；三，石刻一題一畫，較彩繪

更為合理，如「化行中都」、「誅少正卯」、「魯國大治」三幅在彩

繪中僅為一幅。所以，我們可以這樣認為，彩繪應當早於石刻，

跋中「出自成弘間」的說法是比較正確的。

彩繪《聖蹟之圖》繪制的依據主要是《史記·孔子世家》，文

字也多用原作，選擇的是孔子生平中比較重要的行跡，但是著名

的「禮墮三都」、「韋編三絕」、「五乘從遊」、「靈公

郊迎」等却沒有反映，這是不可能的，很可能原本沒有全部保存

下來，今存的只是殘本。

彩繪《聖蹟之圖》有文有贊，但無題，為便於了解內容，參照

石刻例，每幅各加一題。凡石刻有的，均以石刻名為題；石刻無

有的，依據《史記·孔子世家》命名，如「在齊聞韶」、「女樂文

馬」二幅。「丑次同車」二幅，內容不可再分，無法加題，只得標

以（一）、（二）。原畫裝裱成冊，現已散開，無法得知原來排列順

序，只得按照《史記·孔子世家》前後順序排列，未采自《史記

·孔子世家》的「麒麟玉書」、「二龍五老」、「鈞天降聖」、「命名

榮貺」、「跪受赤虹」五幅，按照石刻《聖蹟之圖》的順序插入。

《聖蹟之圖》是我國現存最早、以反映人物事跡為主、具有

完整故事情節的連環圖畫。它圖文並茂，擇要介紹孔子一生的主

要行跡，是一部形象化的孔子編年史。它設色鮮明，繪畫精細，

人物生動傳神，具有較高的歷史價值和藝術價值。

# Foreword

"Pictures of the Sage's Traces" is a picture-story book reflecting Confucius' life-time story.

Confucius, named Kong Qiu, styled Zhohg Ni, was a native of Changping Village in Zouyi in the Lu State (in the present day Nishan to the south-east of Qufu in Shandong) during the Spring and Autumn Period. He was a great thinker, politician and educator in China's history.

Confucius' ancestors were from the Song State's Duke clan. His great-grand father, Fang Shu, moved to the Lu State to escape chaos created by Huadu, and later, his father, Shu Lianghe, turned to be an official in Zouyi of the Lu State. Confucius was born on August 27,551 A.C. (by the present lunar calendar). When he was three, his father died. Since then, his family began to decline. He followed Yan Zhengzai, his mother, to move to the capital. Influenced by his family and the social circumstances, he was modest in learning since childhood. He displayed with utensils to learn the rites, and was hard at study at the age of 15. He was quick at learning and never tied of it or ashamed of learning from the people who were beneath him. He was poor when he was young, and once he held the official title of Weili (to be in charge of warehouse), Chengtian (to be in Charge of livestock) etc.. At his middle age, he started to gather disciples and engaged in educational conducts. He adhered to no discrimination in education among people with different social background and pioneered in running the educational cause by the private individual. He had changed the situation in which education was run by the official government and monopolized by the aristocrats. Thus, he promoted education to be prevailing among the common people. At around 50, Confucius started to be enlisted in political activities, he had held the official titles of Minister of Zhongdu, Minister of the State Construction and Minister of the Punishments. Several years later, he resigned his official title and left for travelling to a series of other states, publicizing his political adherences in seeking for the opportunity to materialize his ideas. Without even stopping long enough to warm his seat, he hurried from one place to another, from State Wei to States Cao, Song, Chen,Cai and Chu. But his advocations were adopted by none of the rulers of these states. In fact, he ran into snags and be foiled everywhere. In his old age, he returned to the Lu State and concentrated on reviewing, finalizing, compiling and studing the books of Shishu, Rites and Music, the Spring and Autumn and Yijing. On February 18, 479 A.C., he died with his noble ideal unfulfilled. He was buried close to the Si River to the north of the City Lu.

During his lifetime, Confucius made great contributions to the mankind and left behind him a rich collection of cultural relics. He collated cultural relics and classics, dedicated himself to education, set a good example for the offsprings in learning knowledge with great eagerness, his meticulus scholarship and the way in combining studing with thinking. His contribution also lies in the fact that he created Confu cianism. He adhered to the idea that the benevolent

should love the people, proposed the doctrine of the mean, persisted in ruling people by virtue and educating them by enlightenment. He opposed tyranny and punishing and killing people wantonly. When Confucius was alive, he was not highly valued by the then rulers and neither was his Confucianism. But later, the Han Dynasty dismissed all the other schools of thoughts only worshipped Confucianism. Ever since the Han, the ruling classes had constantly remoulded Confucius' thinkings and made the doctrine of Confucius and Mencius the orthodox in China's feudal society and Confucius was worshipped as the "Forefather of the Supreme Sage with Great Achievement" and an "Exemplary Master of Virtue and Learning for Generations".

In order to express the respect and cherish the memory of Confucius, from the Han Dynasty and on, people began to create the visible images of him. In 178, the Eastern Han had the Hong Dumen Academy set up in its capital and the academy drew pictures of Confucius and his 72 disciples. And the picture of Confucius paying visit to Lao Zi was also carved on the stones in Wu Liang Temple in Jiaxiang County, Shandong. In the Confucian Temple in Qufu, there were pictures of Confucius with his two disciples standing in attendance with books in hands of the Northern Dynasty and Confucius followed by his ten disciples of the Eastern Wei. In the Northern Song, there was added a copy of fellow-travellers, legendarily painted by Gu Kaizhi of the Jin, together with the picture of miniature figure painted by Wu Daozi of the Tang, picture of conducting lectures and the stone carving of Confucius being the Minister of Punishments. These are the forerunners of the "Pictures of the Sage's Traces".

"Pictures of the Sage's Traces" came into being approximately in the Ming. They appeared in coloured-painting, wood-carving and stone-engraving copies. This is a copy of the coloured one, painted on silk, with 36 pictures, which were mounted on paper book. Each page is 66.2cm wide and 41.4cm high, with the pictures ranging from 57cm to 62cm in width and around 33cm in highness. The painters' names were not given and with the author and the time of painting and coping unknown. There are two postscripts coming before the pictures, one was written in 1729, and it says the book was made between 1465—1505.

Among Qufu's "Pictures of the Sage's Traces", there are stone carvings with accurate date of the 20th year of the reign of Emperor Wan Li. According to records, in Queli, there used to be many pictures of the Sage's traces, they were scattered in all the wing rooms. In the 19th year of the reign of Emperor Wanli, He Chuguang, Patroling Officer of Shandong, proposed that all the wood-carvings should be copied into the stone ones and he built up a Hall of the Sage's Pictures behind the Qin Hall. In the following year, Zhang Yingdeng, Deputy Head of the Department of Justice in Shandong, came to Qufu, he proposed more pictures about the Sage's activities should be included, thus enabling the number mounting to 112. Compared with the stone carving pictures, the coloured "Pictures of the Sage's Traces" has only one extra picture. Apart from this, there are also some minor differences in some of them. The above-mentioned shows that the coloured paintings and the stone carvings have a certain relationship in the same source. There are two possibilities: either they are

are copies of the wood carvings, collected in the ancient Confucian Temple or the coloured paintings are the master copies for the stone ones. But the stone carvings can in no way be the master copies for the coloured paintings. The reasons as follows: 1. The stone carvings are more concentrated, for instance, 'the picture "Being Ashamed of Travelling in the Same Carriage with People Who Didn't Know the Rites Properly", in the coloured paintings there are two about the same subject, but in the stone carvings, it combined the two into one, and selected the scene in which Duke Ling travelled with his wife in the same carriage, Confucius who was left behind and angrily getting on his carriage intending to leave; 2. On each of the stone carving, there is a four-character topic and it is more eye-catching; 3. For the stone carvings, each picture bears one topic, it is more logical. To illustrate, among the stone carvings, there are three separate pictures: "Popularizing Adherences in Zhongdu", "Killing Shao Zhengmao" and "Administering in the State of Lu", but these three appeared on the same picture in the coloured paintings. So we can come to the conclusion that the coloured paintings should be earlier than the stone ones, hence, the postscript is correct in saying that it came into existence during 1465—1505.

The coloured "Pictures of the Sage's Traces" based mainly on "Shiji (Historical Records) & Kongzi Shijia (Confucius' Family)" and the inscriptions are also quoted from the original works and selected parts about the relatively important conducts of Confucius in his lifetime. As the famous events of "Taking Over the Three Cities by Rites", "Reading the Classics Written on the Bamboo Slips so Often, That the Binding Threads were Broken for Three Times", "Comment on How Duke Mu Became Powerful", "Travelling with Five Carriages Following", and "Met by Duke Ling in the Suburbs" are not reflected in the pictures, that seems impossible. There is the great possibility that the original copy was not handed down completely and what we have today is only the remnant copy.

The coloured paintings of "Pictures of the Sage's Traces" bear both the explanation and the assessment, but with no topics. For the convenience of knowing its contents, we have added a topic to each picture by consulting the stone carvings. As long as there is a topic on the stone picture for the same subject, then, it has been copied down. For those which are not named by the stone carvings, they have been named after the stories given in "Shiji & Kongzi Shijia". The original works were mounted and bound into one volume. Unfortunately, the volume was unbound and there is no way in knowing the original sequence. The only solution is to arrange the pictures according to the order depicted in "Shiji & Kongzi Shijia". There are five pictures which are not included in "Shiji & Kongzi Shijia", they are inserted according to the sequence of the stone carvings of "Pictures of the Sage's Traces".

"Pictures of the Sage's Traces" is China's oldest picture-story book in existence today, which has laid stress on depicting people's deeds with complete plots. With both inscriptions and pictures, the book has summarized the major events and Confucius' lifetime and it is a vivid annals of Confucius. The coloured "Pictures of the Sage's Traces" is painted in bright colour, of exquisite painting skill and the figures are so vivid and lifelike. They are of relatively high historical and artistic value.

# 目錄

# Contents

明嘉靖九年釐定祀
典易孔廟像以主然
於藝也短傳以丹青即
然永樂八年賓詔令
繪塑聖賢羣賢衣冠
務就古制是冊制多
精於古其出自成弘
間春即後之人眵譽
欲之餘則珍若斛珠
儻拾禮器之似杳且藏

為尺壁浔覩此羲冠
博帶凝睛橋頼之君
可對語若可步趨
之像低不寶如七尺
珊瑚卽詩云髙山仰
止景行止其懷此
意也夫
昔清雍正己酉午月也
藤園谷程澤光
於邗上之同慧堂

昔司馬氏作史記列

孔子於世家掇拾諸書按年

敘事詳贍淂體俾

宣聖生平昭揭萬古可謂

書中有畫然聖人之思

容第可想像於誦讀之

下而未能晤對於顏面

之間王子欽翁博雅好

古購淂此圖自尼山誕

聖以迄西狩絕筆七十

三年之行藏悉依傷史
記傳諸筆墨奕〻生動
神采焰人又可謂之畫
中有書雖與史記並埀
天壤可也余願後之人
接衣冠瞻視之尊油然
而動私淑之慕想刪訂
纂修之跡殷然而興羡
墙之思睹轍環之勞蹤
知東周之可復悟木鐸

之至教忻斯文之常

存方為善閱此圖者若

第賞其晃旒秀發旌旂

飛揚而置諸几案之上

雜諸鼎彝之間侈為耳

目玩好之物其襄已甚

夫豈王子藏此圖之心

哉

之醮邸

庚戌孟夏題於邗江

絳岩衞支彰

## 1. Praying at Nishan Mountain.

　　Yan Zhengzai, Confucius' mother, prayed in Niqiu Mountain. Afterwards, she gave birth to Confucius. As Confucius' head was low in the crown but high in the part around it, just like the shape of the Niqiu Mountain, hence he was called Kong Qiu and　styled Zhongni.

一　尼山致禱

　　孔子的母親顏徵在在尼丘山上祈禱後，生下兒子孔子。孔子生來頭頂中間低、四周高，像尼丘山的形狀，故起名叫孔丘，字仲尼（參見《史記‧孔子世家》《孔子家語‧本姓解》）。

## 2. A Unicorn with the Heavenly Book.

Before Confucius was born, a unicorn came to his home with a heavenly book in its mouth. There were words in the book, they read:"Son of the God of Water Will Be the Civilian Sage After the Decling State of Zhou". Confucius' mother was curious about it and tied a piece of thread on its horn. Two nights later, the unicorn left. Confucius' mother gave birth to him after 11 months of her pregnancy.

孔子還沒有
出生時，有隻麒
麟在他家裏口吐
天降之書，上面
有文字說：「水
精之子，繼衰周
而素王」。孔子
的母親感到很奇
怪，就用繡紋繫
在麒麟的角上，
隔了兩夜才離去。
孔子的母親懷姙
十一個月才生了
孔子（參見《孔
子集語‧曾子》
引《伏侯古今注》、
《拾遺記》）。

二
麒麟玉書

### 3. Two Dragons and Five Celestial Beings.

Confucius was born in the evening of August 27, 551 A.C.. In that evening, two dragons descended from heaven, circling around to protect his house and five celestial beings descended to his courtyard.

三 二龍五老

魯襄公二十二年（公元前五五一年）十一月庚子（農曆八月二十七），孔子誕生的晚上，有兩條蒼龍自天降下，繞護着他家，五位神僊降到他家院中（參見《孔子集語‧曾子》引《伏侯古今注》。

## 4. The Sage Descending from Heaven.

When Confucius was born, Madam Yan, his mother, heard there was music floating in the air, and a voice saying "The Heaven Senses a Child-sage Is Coming into the World. So It Plays Music to Accompany Him". So Confucius differed from the ordinary people even at his birth. He was distinguished by 49 marks, for instance, he had a wide forehead, a high nose bridge, river-like eyes and sea-shaped mouth, on his chest there were auspicious words.

四　鈞天降聖

孔子出生時，顏氏在房中聽到天上的音樂聲，還聽到空中說：「天感生聖子，故降以和樂之音。」所以孔子生來就與凡人不同，有四十九種標記，如日角月準，河目海口等，胸間還有「制作定世符」的文字（參見《東家雜記》《祖庭廣記》等）。

孔子世家》。

孔子三歲時，父親叔梁紇就去世了。孔子小時玩樂，常常擺上俎豆等禮器，演習禮儀，動作都合乎禮節法度（事見《史記·孔子世家》。

五

俎豆禮容

## 5. Practising the Rites by Displaying Utensils.

Confucius' father died when he was three. He played music since childhood and often practised rites by displaying utensils, which were arranged in the proper etiquette.

孔子既爲委吏
季氏主吏料量
平
嘗曰
豈聖豈仕
長積是司
嘗計當悅
料量遂宜
味主年
次行自
不義乎
所以

## 6. Holding the Official Title of Weili.

After Confucius came of age, once he held the official title of Weili (to be in charge of the warehouse) for Ji Sun Clan. He was very fair in weighing and calculating.

孔子成年後，曾爲季孫氏的委吏（管理倉庫的小官），稱量算數都很公正（事見《史記·孔子世家》）。

# 7. Naming the Son in Memory of the Honour Granted.

Confucius' son was born in 532 A.C.. Duke Zhou of the Lu State granted him a carp, in order to flaunt the bestowal by the monarch, he named his son Kong Li (Li means carp) and styled him Boyu (Yu means fish).

七　命名榮貺

魯昭公十年（公元前五三二年），孔子生了兒子，昭公賜給鯉魚，孔子為了顯耀國君的賞賜，給兒子取名孔鯉，字伯魚（事見《孔子家語・本姓解》）。

## 8. Holding the Official Title of Chengtian.

During his youth, once Confucius held the official position of being in charge of the livestock for the Ji Clan. He had the livestock propagated and increased in number.

八 職司乘田

孔子年輕時，曾爲季氏司職吏（管理苑囿的小官），牲畜繁殖增多（事見《史記·孔家世家》）。

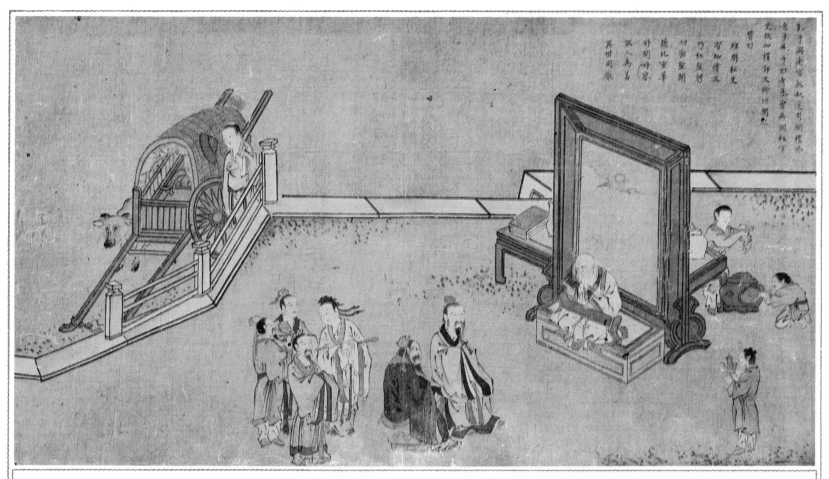

## 9. Learning Rites from Laodan.

Once, Confucius and Nangong Jinshu went together to State Zhou to ask Laozi about the rites, because the latter had held the official position of being in charge of collecting the historical books and was versed with the rites of the State of Zhou.

九　問禮老聃

孔子和南宮敬叔一齊到周地去，向老子問禮，因為老子曾做過周王朝的守藏室之史（管理藏書的史官），熟知周禮（事見《史記·孔子世家》、《孔子家語·觀周》、《莊子·天運》等）。

## 10. Listening to Shao Music in State Qi.

When Confucius was 35 years old, Duke Zhao was defeated by the Clans of Ji Sun, Shu Sun and Meng Sun. The Duke escaped to State Qi with Confucius following him. There, Confucius talked about music with the Grand Master of Qi and listened to the music composed legendarily by Monarch Shun. He was so intoxicated with the music that for three months running, he didn't even know the taste of the food he had taken.

孔子三十五

歲時，魯昭公被
季孫氏、孟孫氏、
叔孫氏打敗，逃
奔到齊國，孔子
也追隨到了齊國。
孔子和齊國太師
談論音樂，聽了
傳說舜作的樂曲
韶樂，沉醉其中，
以至三個月都賞
不出肉的香味來
（事見《史記·
孔子世家》、《論
語·述而》）。

孔子年五十五才得異秦聯奏
全運邦聖華于平子聚三家此攻昭
谷陽故齊人孔子達齊為高昭子家
流此以適于景公到齊人稀之
首三月不知肉咏齊人稀之
詔約
祖述政虎
音造政虎
不聞味麻
乃闘舜拍
聲人問通
神食歌職
魯味為世
何況化享

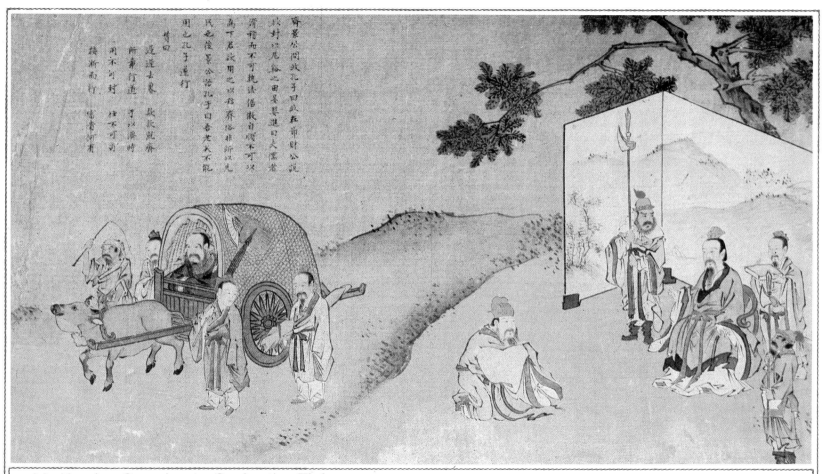

齊景公問政孔子曰政在節財公說
欲封尼谿之田晏嬰進曰夫儒者
滑稽而不可軌法倨傲自順不可以
為下君義用之以稽程齊俗非所以
先民也隆景公語孔子曰吾老失不能
用也孔子遂行

奉曰
遠違吾衆
而弗行道
所以弗行
而不可封
接浙而行
儒者何有

## 11. Yanying Opposing to Confer the Fief.

While Confucius in the State of Qi, Duke Jing asked him how to rule the state, he said the duke should be economical in finance. Duke Jing was so happy that he wanted to confer the fief of Nixi to Confucius, but he was objected to by the high ranking official Yanying. Then Confucius left the State of Qi and returned to the State of Lu.

十一　晏嬰沮封

孔子在齊國，
齊景公問孔子如
何治理國家，孔
子要他節省財力。
齊景公很高興，
想把尼谿的田地
封賜給孔子，但
遭到大臣晏嬰的
反對，於是孔子
離開齊國，返回
魯國。(事見《史
記·孔子世家》、
《孔子家語·弟
子行》)。

## 12. Withdrawing to Review Shishu.

During the reign of Duke Lu, the Ji Sun Clan assumed the Duke title and the high ranking officials took charge of offering sacrifices and going on punitive expeditions. Confucius could not bear to see the situation in which the rites collapsed and the music went out of tune. He seeked for no official position, instead, he cocentrated his efforts on reviewing Shishu and finalizing the rites and music.

十二 退修詩書

魯定公時，季孫氏僭越公室，大臣們掌握了祭祀、征伐等國家政事，孔子看不慣這種禮崩樂壞的局面，不求做官，專心修詩書，定禮樂（事見《史記·孔子世家》等）。

## 13. Meeting the Duke from State Qi in Jiagu.

In the spring of 505 A.C., the monarchs of the States Qi and Lu met in Jiagu. After the presents were exchanged, the musicians from the State of Qi played the music of the four directions. Confucius reasoned that when two monarchs had met, no vulgar music should be played. Duke Jing was forced to withdraw his musicians and dancers, and had the court music played. Then Confucius reasoned that the ordinary men had confused the dukes, and Duke Jing was forced to punish his musicians. Thus making State Lu victorious diplomatically.

十三　夾谷會齊

魯定公十年（公元前五〇〇年）春，齊魯兩國國君相會於夾谷。獻酬後，齊國演奏四方之樂，孔子以兩君相會，不能用夷狄之樂，迫使齊景公撤走樂舞，齊國又演奏宮中之樂，孔子以匹夫惑亂諸侯迫使齊景公處罰樂人。使魯國在外交上取得了一次勝利（事見《史記·孔子世家》、《孔子家語·相魯》）。

定公十年春齊景公會孔子
攝行相事獻俎隉萃蕃有司
方之樂姓棋則誘誡誘而生孔子趨
而進歷階而登篆狄揚言曰吾兩君
為好夷狄之樂何為於此請命有司
卻之萬公心怍揮之而去之有頃齊
司請奏宮中之樂俳優侏儒為戲孔
子趨而進歷階四大夫惡諸侯雷誅
請命有司司加法焉景公懼懼與其竿
戶山製以當守之道苦糊其路而孔子
歸以事故之道教襄人使歸所侵阿鄆千
君放定容齊侯乃歸歸師所侵魯之鄆
陽龍簧田以謝過

## 14. Apologizing by Returning the Land Occupied.

After the meeting in Jiagu, Duke Jing reproached his high ranking officials with discourtesy in diplomatic affairs, for they taught him the ordinary people's mean way. Duke Jing adopted his subjects' suggestion and returned the land of Yun, Wenyang and Guiyin occupied by Qi to State Lu.

十四　歸田謝過

夾谷相會之

後，齊景公責備

大臣們「以夷狄

之道敎寡人」，在

外交上失禮。齊

景公采取臣子的

建議，將過去侵

占的魯國鄆、汶

陽、龜陰之田送

還魯國（事見《史

記·孔子世家》、

《孔子家語·相

魯》）。

## 15. Killing Shao Zhengmao.

In 496 A.C., when Confucius held the title of Minister of Justice, he had Shao Zhengmao, who had created disorder in the state, beheaded. He was in office for three months, in which period the state was in excellent order—no one would pick up and pocket anything lost on the way, men and women were not mixed up and the sellers would ask for no more than their goods' actual value.

十五　誅少正卯

魯定公十四
年（公元前四九
六年），孔子由大
司寇攝行相事，
誅殺了「亂政」
大夫少正卯。參
預國家大事三個
月，路不拾遺，男
女有別，賣東西
的不要虛價，國
家呈現大治的景
象（事見《史記·
孔子世家》、《孔
子家語·相魯》
及《始誅》等）。

## 16. Presenting Female Musicians and Horses.

When State Qi learnt that Confucius was in charge of the state affairs, she worried about that State Lu would become powerful and annex her. So Qi followed Lichu's advice and presented Duke Ding with 80 female musicians and 30 teams of four horses, in an attempt to make the monarch and subjects of State Lu to indulge in excessive amusement to sap their will.

十六　女樂文馬

　齊國聽說孔子執政，擔心魯國稱霸會吞併齊國，采用黎鉏的建議，贈送給魯定公女樂八十人、文馬三十駟，企圖使魯國君臣玩樂喪志（事見《史記·孔子世家》、《孔子家語·子路初見》）。

齊人聞孔子為政懼而
謀沮壞魯國政治。以計
地為割而獻諸先魯祖
之而不行亦惑地獻魯
宇秘故於而舞為二十
卻於是選女子八十人，
道道觀怠於此事孔子
賢曰
黑蠶相聞
紙齊長成
刺鹿遠莫
女樂乃路
師遂正行
始失聖蹤
從矢聖蹤
尼或告遠

## 17. Leaving State Lu for Not Being Given the Sacrificial Meat.

Duke Ai of State Lu was taken in by the Qi people. He went to see the female musicians and stayed with them day and night. He had neglected the state's affairs and forgotten the usual practice of distributing the sacrificial meat to the ministers after the offerings made in the suburb. So Confucius resigned his post and left for travelling to the other states.

十七　因膰去魯

魯君上了齊
人的當，往觀女
樂，終日不歸，怠
惰於國家政事，
郊祭後又沒有按
照慣例向大夫們
分送祭祀的脧肉。
孔子於是辭職出
走，開始周遊列
國（事見《史記·
孔子世家》、《孔
子家語·子路初
見》等）。

## 18. Being Rescued from the Siege by the Kuang People.

After Confucius left State Lu, he went to State Wei, and then on his way from Wei to Chen, he passed by a place named Kuang. As Confucius looked like Yang Hu, who was a native of State Lu and treated the Kuang people brutally. So both Confucius and his disciples were besieged by the Kuang people for five days. Confucius sent his retinue to ask Ning Wuzi of State Wei for help. When he was released, he left the land of Kuang.

十八　匡人解圍

　　孔子離開魯國，從衛國去陳國，路過匡地，魯國的陽虎曾施暴於匡人，孔子長得象陽虎，匡人就把孔子師徒圍拘了五天，孔子派隨從求助於衛國大夫寧武子才解了圍，離開匡地（參見《史記·孔子世家》、《論語·子罕》、《孔子家語·困誓》等）。

孔子去衛過曹適伯為月餘
及子衛士過伯之家
靈公與夫人同車使
孔子為次乘游市孔子曰
吾未見好德如好色
者乞去之
贊曰
倍往莠秦
非力瑶帘
所希仕衛
或可得時
何或後客
德色英好
群城群敬
恐淯吾道

十九　丑次同車
二十　丑次同車

　　孔子離開衛
國，到了蒲地，
一個多月又回到
衛國，寄居在蘧
伯玉家。一天，
衛靈公和夫人坐
在一輛車上，讓
孔子坐在後面的
車上，孔子很生
氣地說：「我從
沒有見過象喜歡
美貌女子一樣喜
歡美德的人呢！」
於是離開了衛國
（參見《史記·
孔子世家》、《論
語·衛靈公》、
《孔子家語·七
十二弟子》等）。

**19. 20. Being Ashamed of Travelling in the Same Carriage with People Who Were Heedless to the Rites.**

Confucius went from State Wei to the land of Pu, and after a month and more, he went back to State Wei again. He stayed with Qu Boyu's family. One Day, when Duke Ling of State Wei sat in the same carriage with his wife and left Confucius sit in the carriage behind his. Confucius said angrily, "I wish there were people who had loved the people of virtue as much as they had loved the beautiful girls." Then he left State Wei.

## 21. The Song People Felling Down the Tree.

In the third year during the reign of Duke Ai of State Lu, Confucius left State Cao for State Song, where he practised the rites under a big tree. Sima Huantui wanted to kill him. First he felled down the tree. Confucius' disciples persuaded him to leave quickly. He said: "The heaven has granted me with such morals, how could Huantui do anything to me?"

二一 宋人伐木

魯哀公二三年，孔子離開曹國到宋國，在大樹下演習禮儀，宋國的司馬桓魋要殺孔子，伐掉了大樹。弟子們勸孔子快走，孔子說：「老天使我有了這樣的品德，桓魋能把我怎麼樣？」〔事見《史記·孔子世家》《論語·述而》等〕。

孔子去衛過曹至於宋與弟子習禮大樹下宋司馬桓魋欲殺孔子拔其樹孔子去弟子曰可以速矣孔子曰天生德於予桓魋其如予何

**22. A Bird Shot Through by an Arrow with a Straw Shaft.**

Confucius went to State Chen and lived in Sicheng Zhengzi's home. One year later, a bird flew into the Chen court and died. It was killed by an arrow with a straw shaft of 0.6 metre long and a stone head. Duke Min sent someone to ask Confucius about it. Confucius said the arrow belonged to Su Shen. After King Wu defeated Zhou, the arrows had been alloted to Chen. Duke Min sent people to the state warehouse and found true to Confucius' words, the arrows were found there.

二二 楛矢貫隼

孔子到陳國，寄寓在司城貞子家。過了一年多，有隼鳥飛集到陳國廷中死去，是被長一尺八寸、制箭桿、石制箭鏃的箭射中的。陳湣公派人去問孔子，孔子說，這是肅慎氏的箭，武王克商以後，曾分給陳國。陳湣公派人到府庫中果然查到這種箭（事見《史記・孔子世家》等）。

孔子遇蒲這裡與衛子擊磬有
蕢磬而遇門曰有心哉擊磬乎
既而曰鄙哉硜硜乎莫己知也
斯已而已矣深則厲淺則揭孔
子曰果哉末之難矣
詩曰
播越學者
欺壞天下　萬行歲春
荷蕢何知　萬間蓍觀
次天下上　紅筆經為

## 23. Adopting State Wei's Way in Beating the Chime Stone.

Confucius went across Pu and came to State Wei. He beat the chime stone together with his disciples. A person, carrying baskets of straws, passed by and said: "The sound is of such profound meaning." A moment later, he said again: "It is a shame that the sound rings stubbonly but couldn't be understood. It will be better if you stop beating it." He quoted the following poem from "Shijing" to persuade Confucius by saying "If the water is deep, then you pass it with clothes on; but if it is shallow, then you pass it by lifting up the bottom of your clothes" (meaning one must act according to the circumstances)

孔子過蒲到
衛國，和弟子們
擊磬，有一個挑
着草筐子的人從
門前經過，便說：
「有深意啊！擊
磬的。」過了一會
又說：「可鄙呀！
磬聲硜硜。這就
罷休好了。」並以
《詩經·匏有苦
葉》中的詩句勸
諭孔子：「水深，
穿着衣裳走過去，
水淺，撩起衣裳
走過去。」（參見
《史記·孔子世
家》、《論語·憲
問》）。

二三

適衛擊磬

## 24. Learning to Play Music from Shixiang.

Confucius learnt to play musical instrument from Master Xiang. He played the same piece of music for ten days. Then Master Xiang advised him to change into something else. Confucius reasoned that he had not understood the meaning behind it, so he kept on. Afterwards, Scholar Xiang persuaded him twice to change the music, yet twice he refused by saying that he had not gotten the aspiration and moral of it. And it turned out later that the music has been composed by King Wen of Zhou.

孔子向師襄
學習彈琴，十日
不更換曲子，師襄
子勸他練習別的
曲子，孔子以還
沒有掌握此曲道
理而推辭。以後
襄子又先後兩次
觀他，他又分別
以沒有了解此曲
志向、爲人作理
由而推辭。後來
才知此曲是相傳
周文王所作的琴
曲《文王操》(事
見《史記·孔子
世家》、《孔子家
語·辯樂》)。

**25. Turning the Carriage Back on the Bank of the Yellow River.**

    As Confucius was not put in an important position in State Wei, so he wanted to see Scholar Zhao Jian in State Jin. When he reached the Yellow River, he was told that State Jin had killed the virtuous Ministers of Dou Mingdu and Shunhua. Facing the river he sighed "A gentleman shouldn't hurt men of his own like." Then he turned back to State Wei.

二五　西河返駕

孔子在衛國得不到重用，想到晉國去見趙簡子，到黃河邊上聽說晉國殺了賢大夫竇鳴犢、舜華，他臨河嘆惜，認為「君子諱傷其類」，便返歸衛國（事見《史記·孔子世家》、《孔子家語·閑誓》）。

## 26. Duke Ling Asking How to Array the Army.

Confucius turned back to State Wei in 493 A.C.. One day, Duke Ling Asked him how to array the army. Confucius answered he didn't know because he was in search of the rites and against war. The duke was unhappy. The next day, when he talked with Confucius, he held up his head and looked at the flying wild goose. As a result, Confucius left State Wei for State Chen.

魯哀公二年（公元前四九三年），孔子回到衛國，一天，靈公問孔子如何排列軍陣。孔子講求禮義，反對戰爭，回答說沒有學過，衛靈公很不高興。第二天，同孔子談話時，靈公仰觀飛雁。孔子於是離開衛國，到陳國去（事見《史記·孔子世家》、《論語·衛靈公》）。

## 27. Zi Lu Asking the whereabouts of the Ferry.

Confucius went from Chen to Cai, then to Yie, and from Yie back to Cai. On his way back, he met Chang Ju and Jie Ni, who were ploughing together. He sent Zi Lu to ask the whereabouts of the ferry. Jie Ni said:"Bad things like the flood running everywhere. With whom can change them? You'd better follow us to escape the filthy society. What good is there to follow Confucius to escape the bad fellows?" With this, they continued with their work.

二七 子路問津

孔子從陳到
蔡又到葉，從葉
返歸蔡國，碰到
長沮、桀溺在一
同耕地，孔子派
子路去打聽渡口。
桀溺說：「象洪水
一樣的壞東西到
處都是，你們同
誰去改變呢？你
與其跟着孔子逃
避壞人，那裏能
跟得上隨我們逃
避這污濁的社會
呢？」說完，仍
舊不停地繼續做
活（事見《史記·
孔子世家》、《論
語·微子》）。

## 28. Out of Food in the State of Chen.

In 489 A.C., State Chu sent for Confucius. The ministers of the States Chen and Cai were afraid that should State Chu offer an important post to Confucius, it would bring danger to the two states. So they dispatched troops together to encircle Confucius and his disciples in the wildness. They were out of grain, and Confucius' followers were so hungry that they couldn't stand up. But Confucius persisted in explaining and reciting Shijing. Later, he sent Zi Gong to State Chu to ask for help. It was not until the reinforcements came that Confucius was rescued.

二八　在陳絕糧

哀公六年（公元前四八九年），楚國派人聘請孔子到楚國去。陳楚的大夫們擔心楚國重用孔子會給陳楚帶來危險，於是共同發兵將孔子師徒包圍在曠野裏。糧食吃光了，跟隨的人餓得起不來，孔子仍然講誦詩書、撫琴歌詠。後來派子貢到楚國，請來救兵，才得以脫身（事見《史記・孔子世家》、《孔子家語・在厄》、《困誓》等）。

## 29. Zi Si Opposing to Confer the Fief.

When Confucius arrived in State Chu, King Zhao intended to bestow the land of Shushe with a length of 350 kilometres on him. But Chu's official Zi Si held that if Confucius had the bestowal, being assisted by his disciples, it would not be conducive to State Chu. Then King Zhao withdrew his original intention and Confucius left State Chu.

二九　子西沮封

孔子到了楚国，楚昭王想把书社之地七百里赐封给他。楚国的令尹子西认为孔子有贤弟子相助，再有了封地，将不利於楚国。楚昭王於是取消了赐封孔子的念头，孔子也离开楚国，返回卫国（事见《史记·孔子世家》）。

楚昭王将以书社地封孔子，令尹子西揶之曰：王之使使諸侯有如子贡者乎？曰：無有。王之辅相有如顏回者乎？曰：無有。王之将率有如子路者乎？曰：無有。王之官尹有如宰予者乎？曰：無有。且楚之祖封於周，號為子男五十里。今孔丘述三五之法，明周召之業，王若用之，則楚安得世世堂堂方數千里乎？夫文王在豊，武王在鎬，百里之君卒王天下。今孔丘得據土壤，賢弟子為佐，非楚之福也。昭王乃止。（事見《史記》卷四十七《孔子世家》）

**30. Composing the Song of Qiu Ling.**

At the age of 68, Confucius lived in State Wei. Ji Kangzi, the Executive Minister of State Lu, sent for Confucius with gifts. Upon turning back to the motherland, Confucius composed the song of Qiu Ling to express his emotions.

三十 作歌丘陵

魯哀公十一年，孔子六十八歲，在衛國。魯國執政大夫季康子派人攜帶禮物請孔子回國。孔子歸國，作丘陵之歌，抒發自己的感慨（事見《孔業子·記問》）。

## 31. Teaching the Rites and Music on the Apricot Terrace.

Confucius finally returned to State Lu and ended his life of a dozen years of travelling around to the other states. But State Lu did not recruit him, and on his part, Confucius seeked for no official title, instead he collated the ancieht documents, wrote preface for book "Shangshu", taught "Liji", reviewed "Shijing", finalized "Yue" and eulogized "Yijin". He taught the above-mentioned to his disciples. He had 3000 disciples. Among them, 72 were well versed in the 6 kinds of arts-Rites, Music, Shishu, Shijing, Yijing and The Spring and Autumn.

三一 杏壇禮樂

孔子回到魯國，結束了十幾年的周遊列國生活，但魯國不用孔子，孔子也不求仕，整理古代文獻，序《書》、傳《禮》、刪《詩》、正《樂》、贊《易》，以詩書禮樂敎育弟子，弟子三千，身通六藝者有七十二人（事見《史記·孔子世家》）。

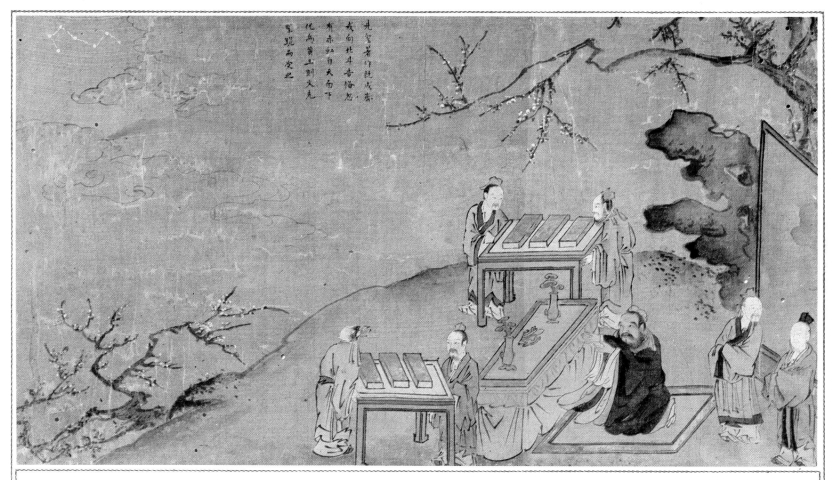

先聖著作既成，齋戒向北斗告備，忽然有赤虹自天而下，化為黃玉，刻之。

## 32. Kneeling Down to Receive the Red Rainbow.

After Confucius completed his works, he lived on vegetarian and prayed to the Big Dipper. Suddenly, a red rainbow flew down from the sky. Then the rainbow turned into a piece of yellow jade with words engraved on it. Confucius knelt down to receive it.

孔子著作既成，齋戒向北斗星告備，忽然有赤虹自天而下，化成黃玉，刻「孔提命作，應法為赤制」，孔子跪拜接受（參見《春秋演孔圖》）。

三一　跪受赤虹

### 33. Hunting in the West and Obtaining a Unicorn.

In the spring of the 14th year during the reign of Duke Ai, people of the State Lu went out hunting and killed a strange animal, which was like the river deer and had horns of fresh. Confucius identified it as a unicorn. A unicorn was considered as a benvent animal. It only appeared when morality and justice were prevailing. And since there were no morality and justice, so the unicorn made its appearance and got killed. Confucius exclaimed, "There are no morality and justice in our state." Hence he stopped compiling the Lu State's historical book "The Spring and Autumn".

三三

西狩獲麟

春，魯國打獵打
死一頭異獸，形
狀象麕，長有肉
角，孔子認爲是
麒麟。麒麟是仁
獸，天下有道才
會出現。現在天
下無道，麒麟出
而被殺，「吾道窮
矣」於是停止了
魯國史書《春秋》
的編寫（參見《史
記·孔子世家》、
《公羊傳》、《孔
子家語·辯物》、
《孔業子·記問》）。

哀公十四年

## 34. Seeing Sacrificial Offerings Between Two Columns in Dream.

In the 16th year of the reign of Duke Ai, Confucius was seriously ill. When Zi Gong went to see him, Confucius asked why he had come so late, and sang sadly: "Mountain Taishan is shrinking; The roof beam is decaying; The sage is withering." Tears came down his face as he sang it. Confucius said he had seen sacrificial offerings between two columns in dreams, which resembled the Rin people's funeral practice. So he thought he was going to die. He died on February 18.

三四 夢奠兩楹

哀公十六年，孔子病重，子貢拜見，孔子問子貢爲什麼來得這麼晚，並傷心地唱道：「泰山其頹乎！梁木其壞乎！哲人其萎乎！」淚隨歌下。孔子說，昨天夢中坐奠兩楹之間，很象殷人殯喪的制度，認爲自己快要死了。四月乙丑（農曆二月十八日（去世）事見《史記·孔子世家》、《禮記·檀弓上》等）。

## 35. Having Fulfilled the Duties and Parting from Each Other.

After Confucius died, he was buried on the bank of River Si to the north of the Lu State's capital. His disciples were in mourning for three years. Then they parted with each other and left. Only Zi Gong remained behind to guard the tomb for another three years in a hut.

孔子死後埋葬在魯國都城以北的泗河邊上，弟子服喪三年，相別而去。獨有子貢在墓側結廬守墓六年才離去（事見《史記·孔子世家》、《孟子·滕文公上》）。

三五 治任別歸

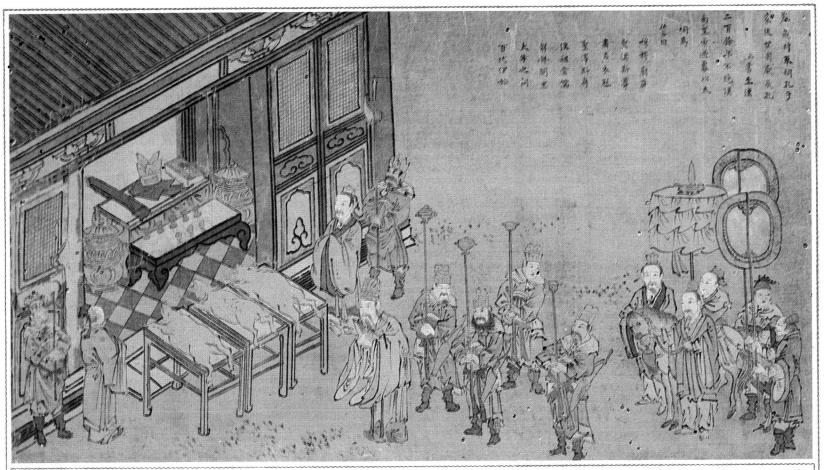

**36. Emperor Liu Bang of the Han Dynasty Offering Sacrifices.**

Ever since Confucius' death, each year, people would offer sacrifices to his tomb on special occasions. And Confucius' old house was changed to be a temple to collect the clothes, hats, musical instruments, carriages and books used by Confucius during his lifetime. When Emperor Liu Bang of the Han Dynasty passed by Qufu, he also worshipped Confucius by offering the sacrificial pig, ox and sheep.

三六　漢高祀魯

孔子死後，人們每年按時祭祀孔子墓。孔子故居被改作廟宇，保存着孔子生前使用過的衣、冠、琴、車、書。漢高祖劉邦經過曲阜，也以太牢（豬、牛、羊三牲）祭祀孔子（事見《史記·孔子世家》）。

# 後　記

　　曲阜孔府是孔子嫡長孫的簡署。兩千多年來，歷代王朝在尊崇孔子的同時也澤及後人，對孔子的嫡孫備加優渥恩寵，賜以爵位，養以俸祿，直至冊封爲世襲罔替的「衍聖公」，使之成爲我國歷史上沿續時間最長的貴族世家。而歷代孔子嫡孫恪守「詩禮傳家」的祖訓，潛心詩書，注意搜集保存禮器法物，使孔府藏有大量的珍貴文物，尤以孔子畫像、衍聖公及夫人肖像、元明衣冠、商周銅器等著稱。我們擬計劃分類選編出版，以供海內外人士存賞。《聖蹟之圖》是其中的一册，其他各册以後將陸續出版。

# Postscript

The Confucius Mansion in Qufu was the official office of Confucius' direct descendents. In the past 2000 years and more, while the rulers of different dynasties worshipped Confucius, they had adored his offsprings as well. They had bestowed great favour on his direct descendants and indulged them. The descendants were confered on official titles, and granted official's salaries. Finally, they were confered on the hereditary title "Duke Yansheng", which made them the aristocratic family with the longest history in China's history. And the descendants of different dynasties strictly adhered to their ancestor's teaching of learning the poems and the rites, they concentrated on studing the poem books and paid attention to collecting the sacrificial vessels and musical instruments. Due to all this, there is a great quantity of valuble cultural relics kept in Confucian Mansion.

Among the collections, the particularly famous ones are Confucius portraits, costumes and hats, portraits of the Dukes of Yansheng and the bronze vessels of the States of Shang and Zhou. For hundreds of years, these relics have been revealed to no outsiders. We intend to sort out and compile them in a planned way. So the people at home and abroad is one of the successive volumes. The others will be published in succession, and in the end, we will put all the volumes into an anthology.

英文翻譯　馬秀卿

責任編輯　劉魁勝

孔府文物選

# 聖 蹟 之 圖

山東省曲阜市文物管理委員會供稿

孔祥林　孔繁銀　執筆

關啟生　王玉珍

龐　守　義　拍攝

山東友誼出版社出版發行

（地址：中國·山東省濟南市勝利大街 39 號　郵编：250001）

濟南新華印刷廠印刷

\*

787×1092 毫米　16 開本　3.25 印張　16 千字

1989 年 6 月新 1 版　2005 年 4 月第 11 次印刷

**ISBN** 7—80551—114—4/J·13

定價：18.00 圓